Walkabout York

A guided tour through a historic city

by
Ivan E Broadhead

Meridian Books

INTRODUCTION

Trying to explore a city, especially one as fascinating as York, can be a frustrating task if your time is limited. Every wrong turning, every retraced step, fritters away your precious time, makes you miss sights worth seeing, and leaves you tired and unsatisfied.

Since no less a person than the Queen has adopted the practice of walkabouts when visiting important cities, and in view of the increasing urge for visitors to leave their motor cars and explore on foot, I decided to produce a simple and clear guidebook that would give the visitor an intimate guide to one of the most attractive cities in Britain. The aim was to design a book so easy to follow that you could use every valuable minute to see and explore on foot some of the details that give York its charm. The map on pages 4 and 5 depicts the route, the numbers indicating the location of some of the features that I have described in the text.

I hope that you will feel that *Walkabout York* has helped you to savour more fully the delights of this beautiful and historic city — and when you get home you will have a pleasant reminder and souvenir of your visit.

For the many schoolchildren who visit the city each year I hope that it will make an interesting start to any projects you may carry out and will awaken your interest in exploring the city even further.

The length of the complete walk is 2⅓ miles (3.75 km) but I have described a detour which will enable you, if you wish, to reduce the distance to about 1¾ miles (2.8 km).

Ivan E Broadhead

Note to the Second Edition

Despite its historic nature York is ever-changing and new features and facts about its past are forever being discovered. I have therefore taken this opportunity to revise and update *Walkabout York* by incorporating some new information and photographs.

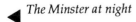 *The Minster at night*

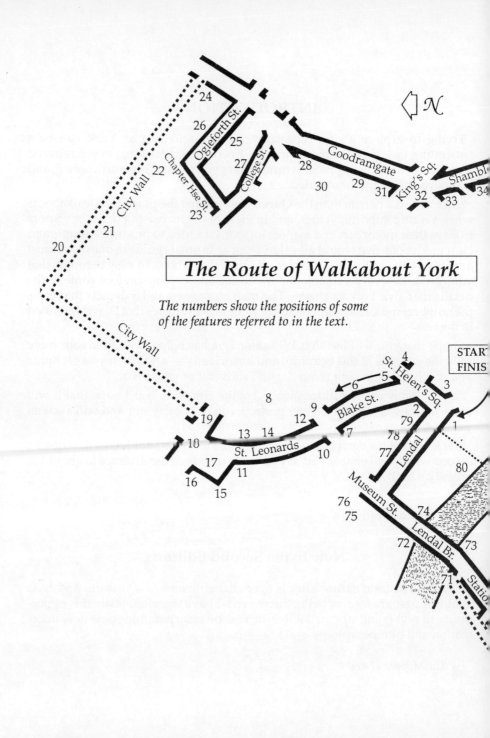

The Route of Walkabout York

The numbers show the positions of some
of the features referred to in the text.

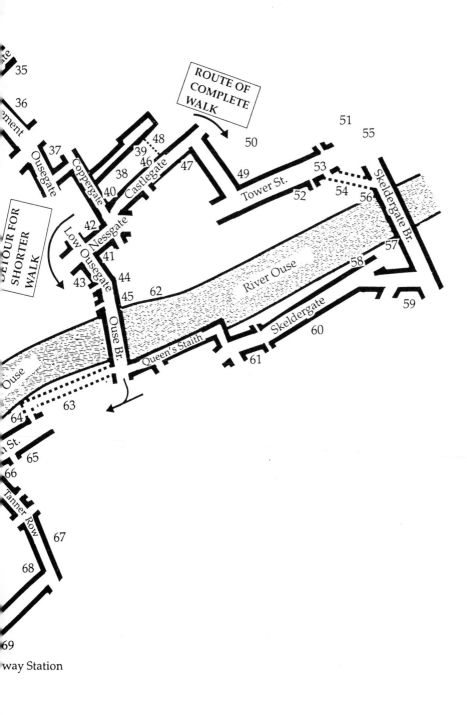

OUR WALK starts at the **Mansion House (1)**, designed by Richard Boyle, Earl of Burlington and completed in 1726. York has the honour of being the first city to have an official residence for its Lord Mayor — London copied the concept ten years later.

Although the appearance of the Mansion House suggests a three-storied building there are, in fact, only two storeys — the upper windows create a deception. It has an imposing stateroom on the upper floor as well as a large dining room on the ground floor, an extremely valuable collection of antique silver plate and many portraits of historic interest. Among the civic plate is a gift from a rich eccentric, Marmaduke Rawdon, who bequeathed in his will of 19 February 1668 'a silver chamber pott of the value of tenn pounds'. During his year of office the Lord Mayor lives here.

Doorknocker on the Mansion House

Stand with your back to the unusual lion door-knocker and look to your left at the imposing stone building by G T Andrews (1840) inscribed 'Yorkshire Insurance Co. established MDCCCXXIIII' which now houses the General Accident Co. Hereabouts was the **Praetorian Gate (2)**, the principal entrance to the city in Roman times. The original date is uncertain but it was probably rebuilt around AD300. It commanded the entrance to the Praetorium whence Petillius Cerealis and Julius Agricola had once directed the Roman legions, Emperor Severus concerted his plans for the government of the Northern territories, and where the great Constantine was first acclaimed Emperor on the death — in York — of his father Constantius.

The great gate with two arches each having a roadway about 20 feet wide and 50 feet in length stood partly across the present insurance office entrance and partly across the square.

Set in the York Stone footpath beside the bank is a plaque inscribed 'THIS STONE WAS LAID BY HER ROYAL HIGHNESS THE DUCHESS OF KENT to mark the repaving of St Helens Square 22nd April 1989.'

The **neo-Georgian development (3)** on your right stands on the site of the former Harker's Hotel, built 1870, demolished about 1928 and said in 1873 to be 'largely patronised by American visitors'. Betty's Café and Tea Rooms, acquired in 1936 by Frederick Delmont, had the interior modelled after the

SS Queen Mary. This was changed during wartime but was restored to the original art deco of the liner in 1984. Among relics is a mirror signed by hundreds of wartime aircrew including Americans, Canadians and Australians.

The two Victorian gas lamps on black columns were restored and installed in April 1989. Gas replaced oil for public lighting in 1824 and the first electric lights appeared in the streets around 1900. There are about seventeen gas lamps left in the city.

Walk forward to the left hand side of St Helen's Square. Once known as Cuckold's Corner, it was created in 1745 to allow better access to Blake Street. At the right hand corner is Davygate, a thoroughfare for over eight centuries, named after David le Lardiner, clerk of the royal kitchens in the reign of King Stephen (1135). The title of King's Lardiner was hereditary and his hall in Davygate was granted by the Crown in return for keeping the jail in Galtres Forest,

West Front of the Minster

distraining for the King's debts in the city, and providing venison and meats for the royal table. He was entitled to take a weekly tribute from every butcher, baker and fishmonger.

Ahead is the parish church of **St Martins with St Helen (4)** which serves as the civic church and in medieval times was the glassmakers guild church. Their arms are in one window, but the chief glory is the stained glass in the west window which dates from the fifteenth century and shows figures of St Helen, the Virgin Mary as Queen of Heaven, Edward the confessor, and St William of York. A memorial in the east end of the south aisle commemorates two sisters who lived in the reigns of seven sovereigns. Adjacent is the entrance to Stonegate, one of the city's oldest streets, having been the Via Praetoria in the Roman Camp from AD71 onwards. Some of the best examples of fifteenth and sixteenth century domestic buildings survive here.

Shop entrance at corner of Blake Street

8

The doorway of the **sheepskin shop (5)** at the corner of Stonegate and Blake Street is a fine example of Victorian cast-iron work from Walker's Iron foundry. It was occupied several years before his death in 1771 by the famous clock maker Henry Hindley. In March 1731 the Corporation granted him the freedom of the city 'in consideration of his making and presenting a very good and handsome eight-days clock and case to the Lord Mayor's house, and another for the common hall, and taking care of the same for one year'.

The bank building opposite, erected in 1827, is on your left as you walk up Blake Street. This street was called Blaicastret in 1108 and may mean 'the street where bleaching is carried on'. About two centuries ago it was only wide enough to permit one-way traffic, 'which was found very inconvenient to the company going to and returning from the Assembly Rooms'. It was widened in 1764 and improved since.

A few yards forward, the premises under the projecting clock was a **sixteenth century mansion (6)**.

On the left at the junction with Museum Street are the **Assembly Rooms (7)**. This building was erected by public subscription (1730-1736) to the design of Richard Boyle. The foundation stone was laid by the Lord Mayor in March 1730 in the presence of 'all the gentlemen in the town'. It formed one of the fashionable centres of Georgian England and enjoyed a reputation similar to that of Bath and Norwich. The central hall is similar in style to the Egyptian Hall in London's Mansion House. It measures 112 feet by 40 feet, the roof being supported by forty-eight Corinthian columns. The hall was described in the *York Courant* at the time as being designed for all 'public diversions, such as assemblies, concerts of music, etc . . . and in case a crowned head should ever grace this place, there will be a gallery all round on the outside, where people may look in at the windows and see all that passes in the inside'.

Look to your right up Duncombe Place at the famous and superb view of the **Minster (8)** west front. It is but a short detour if you wish to visit this gem and there are many books available describing its treasures.

The very narrow **Lop Lane (9)**, so-named because it was flea-infested in 1198, was widened in 1864 and renamed after the Hon. Augustus Duncombe, Dean of York (1838-1880) whose vision, energy and generosity brought about the change.

The original purpose of the ornate brick building on your right is revealed by a stone carving of a coat of arms and YORK DISPENSARY over the central arch. Costing nearly £6,000 it was built in 1899 to the design of Edmund Kirby of Liverpool.

Cross the road carefully at the traffic lights, staying on the left, and enter St Leonards Place.

St Leonards Place was constructed by the Corporation in 1839 to provide a more direct route from St Helens Square to Bootham, and in the process about 300 feet of medieval wall between Bootham Bar and the Multiangular Tower in Museum Gardens (which we shall see later) was removed for the **crescent-shaped terrace (10)** which now houses corporation offices. These are the city's only, but successful, example of Regency urban design, later in date than southern counterparts — 'elegant houses after a London style' as one historian wrote. At the end, in a small piece of garden area, are the remains of the **ancient wall (11)** which formed a portion of the defences of the legionary fortress of Eboracum, built around AD300 by the Roman Emperor Constantius Chlorus who died here six years later.

On your right, at the junction of Duncombe Place with St Leonards Place, is the **Red House (12)**, built on the site of the gate-house of St Leonard's Hospital (c. 1718) by Sir William Robinson. Before deciding to erect the present Mansion House in 1724 the Corporation tried to buy the Red House for the purpose, but negotiations failed. In the wall of this house, which fronts St Leonards Place, are many stones which almost certainly formed part of the wall which enclosed the hospital precincts. Here lived Dr John Burton, the prototype of Dr Slop in Laurence Sterne's *Tristram Shandy*. Note the nineteenth century torch extinguisher on the right hand side of the door-knocker, a reminder of the days before street lighting.

Sir William Robinson was Lord Mayor in 1700 and was the great-great-grandfather of Earl de Grey who died in 1859 aged 78 and in whose honour, by a coincidence, the **de Grey Rooms (13)** at the opposite end of St Leonards place on the same side of the street were named. Built 1841-2 as an officers mess for the Yorkshire Hussars they have round headed windows with pediments.

In between is the **Theatre Royal (14)** which was originally erected about 1750 by Joseph Baker who leased the site from the Corporation and rebuilt it in 1765. In 1818 it was lighted with wax candles placed in glass chandeliers of a novel form which prevented the wax from falling on the heads of the audience in the pit — 'a nuisance which has formerly been much complained of'. The present facade was erected in 1880 and since modified by an extension and reconstruction completed on 20 December 1967. Notice, on the front, carvings of the heads of Hamlet, Falstaff, Elizabeth I, Lady Macbeth and Titania beneath William Shakespeare.

Only a few more strides and you are in Exhibition Square with immediately on your left the gate leading to the **Kings Manor (15)** built c.1280 as a residence for the Abbot of St Mary's Abbey. Enlarged c.1460 by Abbot Sever, the Kings Manor received its new name and a new function after the Reformation and the failure of the Pilgrimage of Grace in 1536. It became the headquarters of the Council of the North which lasted about a hundred years until the Civil War. Henry VIII, Charles I and Charles II stayed here. It was occupied by the Earl of

Arms of Kings Manor

Strafford 1628 to 1640, and the artist Francis Place (1650-1728) also lived here. First to live here as Lord President of the Council of the North was Robert Holgate, later Archbishop of York. Henry VIII and Queen Catherine Howard stayed here for three weeks in 1541. One of the rooms still retains its Tudor entrance, a chimney piece and a plaster frieze of the period. In 1603 Lord Burleigh as president received James I on his journey from Scotland. A later president, Lord Sheffield, obtained from the Crown in 1616 a grant of £1000 towards the cost of converting the building into a royal palace. He spent £3300.

Note the coat of arms over the main doorway, with the initials C.R. for Charles Rex, the executed king, at the top, and the N in Mon the wrong way round.

In 1692 an alderman of the city rented the building and converted it into dwelling houses, warehouses and shops. In 1837 it was converted into a school for the blind, and in 1957 became part of the University of York.

The City Art Gallery

Adjacent is the imposing **Art Gallery (16)**, designed by Edward Taylor, which is open to the public. It dates from 1879 when it was the Yorkshire Fine Art and Industrial Association. Outstanding in the collection of paintings is the Lycett Green bequest of European masters. This consists of 120 pictures from the fourteenth to

11

William Etty R.A.

nineteenth centuries. Two painted scenes on the gallery facade depict the death of Leonardo da Vinci, and Michaelangelo carving the statue of Moses. The carved faces depict architect John Carr (1723-1807), sculptor John Flaxman (1775-1843), Minster organist William Cammidge (1735-1803) and painter William Etty (1787-1849).

In front of the gallery there is also a **statue (17)** of William Etty R.A. born in York who was elected a Royal Academician in 1828. At his feet is a small version of Bootham Bar which you can see across the square. This is in memory of his successful bid to stop demolition of part of the city walls in the nineteenth century. In front are the illuminated fountains given to the city in 1971 by the Civic trust to commemorate the 1900th anniversary of the foundation by the Romans. Stand with your back to these and enjoy one of the most famous views of the city. Beside the **archway (18)** on your left is a plaque which reads: 'This gateway was broken through the Abbey wall

Exhibition Square

July 1503 in honour of the Princess Margaret, daughter of Henry VII who was the guest of the Lord Abbot of St Mary's for two days on her journey to the north as the bride of James IV of Scotland'. The road to the left goes to Bootham — the name derives from the old West Scandinavian word Buthum — 'at the booths' — implying a district of humble or temporary dwellings. Jurisdiction over Bootham was hotly disputed between the city and St Mary's Abbey. The main road out of the city to the north, it is on the line of the Roman road which was hereabouts marked by the site of the Porta Principalis, or North Western

Margaret's Arch

Gate, of the Roman fortress. The foundations of this fortress as rebuilt c.AD300 lie just below ground.

The roadway immediately ahead is Gillygate which derived its name from the church of St Giles which stood at the northern end of the street on your left. It was declared redundant in 1547 and taken down about that time. The square itself was created out of a corner of St Mary's Abbey grounds known as Bearpark's Garden.

Cross the road carefully at the traffic lights for the next stage of the walk which involves climbing steps on the right hand side of **Bootham Bar (19)** — but before doing so have a closer look at the structure from ground level.

Probably the most attractive of the bars, Bootham Bar is hemmed in by later, especially eighteenth century buildings: its flight of steps gives access to the walls. The barbican was removed in 1832 but public feeling ensured the survival of the bar itself. The portcullis inside was saved similarly fifty years later.

Bootham Bar

Bootham Bar was the main entry from the north and the Forest of Galtres in olden times. Armed guards were stationed here to conduct travellers through the forest and protect them against wolves. The royal arms were taken down

City walls

in 1650 when Cromwell passed through against Scotland. The heads of the three rebels were exposed here for attacking the restored monarchy in 1663.

Bootham Bar was erected on Roman foundations in the twelfth century and enlarged in the thirteenth century and later. The interior was remodelled in 1719 and rebuilt in stone in 1832. The portcullis still remains. In 1501 it was ordered that a great door-knocker should be fixed to the oak doors of the bar and that 'Scottish persons who were wishful to enter York should knock first'.

From the bar walk along the walls which run north-east following the line of Gillygate. At the point where the wall (all this time following the Roman fortress wall) turns sharply south-east, stands the **northern angle tower** (20), greatly enlarged at the beginning of this century. Its earliest name was Bawing Tower, and in the fifteenth century it was called Frost Tower after William Frost, five times Lord Mayor. In 1622 it was sometimes known as Robin Hood Tower.

It has only been possible to enjoy this walk along the summit of the walls since the restoration of 1887-9 when the supporting arches were added. There are five towers along this stretch, three of which are demi-hexagonal and were probably added in the late fourteenth or fifteenth century. The second tower from the bar has a circular gun port of about 1440 near its base.

Running parallel with the south-east section is Lord Mayor's Walk, called by that name about 1700 but probably originally a street in the twelfth century suburb of Newbiggin. It runs along the outer ditch, here preserved in a condition most like its original form.

Bronze plaque on the city walls

14

Look out for a bronze plaque on the inside parapet of the walls as the top of Monk Bar comes into view. This reads: 'This tablet was placed here by the council of the City of York October 1898 to record that this portion of the wall (371 Linl yds) was in the year 1889 restored to the city by Edwin Gray who served the office of Lord Mayor in 1898'. This resulted from a claim from Gray that he ·owned part of the wall and rampart. Here too can be seen two depressions in the rampart, one marking the site of a destroyed tower, the other indicating the position of the Roman north-east gate — Porta Decumana — and its Norman successor. The lines of the Roman streets approaching it are preserved inside the walls by Chapter

The Treasurer's House

House Street and outside by Groves Lane, now only a narrow alley which you can see across Lord Mayor's Walk.

From this stretch of wall walk there are superb views of the Minster's protected unchanging northern side, **Dean's Park (21)**, **Gray's Court (22)**, and of the seventeenth century **Treasurer's House (23)** which is open to the public.

In Dean's Park the medieval stone tracery of the Minster's great West Window, with its Heart of Yorkshire motif, is buried in a shallow excavation for safe keeping. Six hundred years exposure to the elements had taken its toll and it was replaced in 1989 by a window of French Lepin stone.

The Treasurer's House stands on the site of the Roman Imperial Barracks, of which traces remain. It was the residence of the Minster Treasurer, the first, Randalphus, being appointed in 1100. The present house contains work of the thirteenth century and is believed to have been rebuilt by Archbishop John le Romeyne in the fourteenth century. The office of Treasurer ceased at the Dissolution and Edward VI gave the house to the Protector Somerset who sold it to Archbishop Holgate. Various kings have been entertained here, and Elizabeth Montague, 'Queen of the Bluestockings', was born here in 1718.

Monk Bar

15

Minster Court

Laurence Sterne also stayed here. It was presented to the nation in 1930 and is floodlit at night.

Descend the steps through the narrow side passage at **Monk Bar (24)** and turn right for a slight detour to look at the imposing front of the loftiest (63 feet) and strongest of the medieval gateways to the city.

The vaulted chambers above were the Freeman's Prison. The arms of England are quartered with those of France on the outer side of the bar. The original portcullis still remains.

This bar is on the line of the Roman Wall and was erected on Roman foundations in the thirteenth century, and enlarged in the fifteenth century. The barbican was removed in 1825 and the bar completely restored in 1953 and strengthened in 1979. At first called Monk Gate Bar it was built as a self-contained fortress with every floor defensible if others were captured. The lower three storeys are vaulted in stone and so are fireproof, and the stairs leading to each floor in the thickness of a side wall are so placed that an enemy must cross a room to reach the next stair.

Features to note on the outer facade are the doorways to the barbican and the gallery supported on an arch from which missiles could be dropped through holes, now blocked, on attackers below. The coats of arms below decorated canopies are the Plantagenet royal arms (before the nineteenth century restoration they bore the many *fleur de lys* of Edward III or Richard II) and the arms of the city.

Return to the foot of the steps with the bar behind you and walk forward a few paces past a narrow courtyard on your right called Monk Bar Court, formerly Elbow Lane. A few more steps bring you to a right turn into Ogleforth where you will see on your left a restored ornate **town house (25)** of medieval date. Opposite, behind the iron gates with JW monograms and the dates 1675 and 1983, are eleven almshouses around a **courtyard (26)** featuring a limestone dolphin. They were provided by the Jane Wright charity, founded in 1675 to help 'poor widows and housekeepers' and were opened by HRH The Duchess of Kent on 28 November 1983.

The street name probably enshrines the personal Danish name of 'Ugel', and

St William's College

Doorway to St William's College

in 1109 it was known as Ugelford. Stretching across this street about 35 yards from the corner of Chapter House Street once stood one of the four gates leading into Minster Yard. Gray's Court, which faces you as you walk down Ogleforth, was originally part of the adjoining Treasurer's House which stands in Minster Yard. The office of Treasurer was instituted by Archbishop Thomas (1070-1100) and continued until 1547 when the last treasurer resigned, giving the unanswerable reason for so doing that no treasure remained!

Turn left into College Street which in 1736 bore the name of Little Alice Lane 'from a diminutive woman who once lived here'. Long before that time it was called Vicar Lane from the fact that it led from the Minster to the collegiate hall of the vicars-choral in Bedern. The present name is due to **St Williams College (27)** which stands on your left about midway down the street. To the right of the Minster Yard is the magnificent east end of the Minster and a little further round is a plaque that commemorates the fact that 'Her Majesty Queen Elizabeth the Second walked from the West Door of the Minster along this way to the Treasurer's House after she had distributed the Royal Maundy on March 30th 1972.'

St Williams College is dedicated to William Fitzherbert, nephew of King

17

Our Lady's Row

Stephen and a great grandson of William the Conqueror. He was Archbishop of York in 1153, and when he made his first official entry into York as its Archbishop the crowd that assembled to welcome him was so great that as they passed over Ouse Bridge — then an old wooden bridge — it collapsed and many fell into the water, but no lives were lost.

The college was erected between 1465 and 1467 under letters patent granted by Edward IV to George Nevill, Bishop of Exeter, and his brother Richard, Earl of Warwick. (The Kingmaker), as the home of the chantry priests of the cathedral. In 1642 it was the residence of Sir Henry Jenkins and when King Charles I moved his court from London to York he set up his printing press here. Twelve carved oak figures representing the labours of the months decorate the cantilevered roof of the inner courtyard. A fine sundial is on your right as you walk forward to the half timbered building which bridges the street. It is all that remains of a covered way which Richard II allowed the vicars-choral to build so that they could cross from their home in Bedern to Minster Yard without being molested. The National Trust shop is where the 'Railway King' George Hudson carried on his business as a draper over a century ago until the more lucrative task of creating railways absorbed his attention.

Cross the road into Goodramgate with the **Cross Keys Inn (28)** on your right.

The earliest record of the name Goodramgate appears in 1154 in the form of Gutherungate and it clearly enshrines the Danish personal name Gutherum — but this was not the same Gutherum who led the Danish host which King Alfred defeated in AD878. When and why Goodramgate was constructed in place of the Porta Decumana is a mystery. Probably somewhere on your left stood the Domus Palatina of the Romans — the Palace House in which Emperor Severus lived and subsequently died in AD211.

Notice the carved cross keys of St Peter and the date 1904 on the side of the inn. The sagging half timbered Four Seasons Restaurant building overhanging the pavement on your left dates from 1485. At the turn of the eighteenth century

18

it was the home of the Buckle family. Young Marmaduke was crippled and when his disability became too much to bear he hanged himself from one of the oak beams — which provides an incumbent ghost. Before he died he scratched an inscription into the plaster of one of the first floor walls: 'Marmaduke Buckle/1698/1715/17'.

Next to the restaurant is the Anglers Arms followed by the sixteenth century Wealden Hall whose overhanging gable bears the inscription 'TIA 1700'.

Further down on your right is **Our Lady's Row (29)**, the oldest surviving houses in the city built in 1316 in the churchyard of Holy Trinity to endow a chantry of the blessed Virgin Mary. They are said to be among the oldest in England and are more or less in their original condition.

Indian boy

At the western end of the row, and easily missed, is a rosy brick arch of 1766 hung with iron gates made in the year of Waterloo. Once through them and into Holy Trinity's small churchyard you are in a haven of calm. **Holy Trinity Church (30)**, founded in the first half of the twelfth century contains architecture of the thirteenth and fourteenth centuries with woodwork and pews of the seventeenth and eighteenth centuries. It is a good example of how a church was arranged after the Reformation. The stained glass over the altar was the gift of John Walker, Rector, and is late Perpendicular (1470-1489) — a rare date in York glass. Also over the altar are gold-lettered boards displaying the Lord's Prayer and Exodus Chapter X. The church wardens' accounts contain some fascinating entries including the spending of half a crown (12½p) on bell ringing when Charles II was proclaimed, and a shilling (5p) paid out to a widow of a minister killed by a thunderbolt.

Return to Goodramgate and turn right to pass the **White Swan (31)** which dates back to 1703, but there is thought to have been a pub called Sandhill Inn here much earlier in a complex of about nine buildings which have been altered and extended many times.

Holy Trinity Church

The Shambles

Two wings were lost in 1775 when the Corporation widened the street which was 'excessively narrow' at this point. In 1983 extensive renovation — which won an RIBA Festival of Architecture Award — revealed some fine examples of timber-frame construction and two enormous inglenook fireplaces, one so large it has a passageway running through it.

A few more steps bring you to the junction of Low Petergate to your right. The view up the narrow streets to the bulk of the Minster — St Peter's, which results in the name — is spectacular and famous. Notice immediately around the corner the bizarre figure of an Indian boy which adorned the upper storey of a tobacconist for a couple of centuries to identify the business for the illiterate.

Ahead of you is Church Street, formerly Girdlergate, so-named back in 1360 when the making of sword-belts, key-belts and the like was carried on here. Directly ahead on the left is Colliergate — the charcoal dealers street. Cross the road into Kings Court and the right hand side of Kings Square.

Gravestones (32) are all that remain of the former churchyard of Christ Church which once was the dominating feature here. Its full title was 'The Church of the Holy Trinity in the King's Court, commonly called Christ Church' — a name that immediately suggests you are standing very near to where the kings of Northumbria and of the Danish Kingdom of York had their residence for a considerable period between AD626 and 954, or possibly for all of that time. No king of England since the country became one kingdom has ever had a permanent residence in York. Egil Skallagrim, an Icelandic warrior and bard of the tenth century in a saga composed after visiting York mentions 'King's Garth' in the city. The churchyard originally covered most of the present square and the church was taken down in 1937. The haymarket was held

Wesley window

20

here in the eighteenth and early nineteenth centuries.

At the corner and to your right is Newgate — so called back in 1337 and possibly much earlier — but whose origins are unknown. Before proceeding down the Shambles detour a few paces along Newgate past Pump Yard to look at the building on the right with its one small mullioned window, barred with iron which lends confirmation that it was once a **prison (33)**. This is the building which John Wesley frequently refers to in his diary as 'the oven'. Capable of holding about 120 people it was from 1753 the centre of Methodism in the city. The upper storey was destroyed by fire many years ago.

Undoubtedly one of the best known features of York is the Shambles. This narrow street, where the upper storeys of medieval houses almost touch each other across the pedestrians below, gives a vivid idea of fifteenth and sixteenth century York. This is the ancient street of the butchers of York, mentioned in the Domesday Book. It takes its name from 'Shamel', meaning the stalls or benches on which the meat was displayed — later versions of which can still be seen. It was rebuilt about 1400 when it assumed its present character.

Behind the row on your right the open air market is now held, glimpses of which can be seen through the connecting passages.

Look out on your right for the house of **Margaret Clitheroe (34)** who was made a saint on 25 October 1970. She was the wife of a butcher who died because she would not deny the Catholic faith. Born in 1556 and married at the age of 15, she lived here and kept a small room to hide priests from persecution. But she was arrested, tried at the assizes and crushed to death on 25 March 1586.

Just before you reach the junction with Pavement bear left through a narrow passage which takes you to Whipmawhopmagate, the shortest street in the city. Known in 1505 as Whitnourwhatnourgate it was later changed into the present

WHIP - MA - WHOP - MA - GATE

name, possibly because of the whipping of petty criminals. A pillory was once kept nearby and possibly a whipping cart too.

Turn right past St Crux church room. The churchyard of St Crux once projected some way across the present street and in front were houses called Hosier Row. In 1769 these and the churchyard were removed for the extension of Pavement: in 1881 the church was closed and in 1887 demolished when the small parish hall was erected on part of the site.

Opposite is Fossgate, the name of which occurs as early as AD112. Probably part of a Roman road which led to Brough across the Humber, thence to Lincoln and the south, it crosses the river Foss which resulted in the name. In it is the

All Saints Church

entrance to the **Guild Hall (35)** of the 'Fellowship of Mercers and Merchant Adventurers of York' from the fourteenth century to the present day.

Turn right and walk forward along Pavement; possibly so-called because it was the first street to be paved. Many of the city's wealthiest merchants have resided here, and a typical example is the Herbert family whose **house (36)**, practically unaltered since its erection, stands opposite the lower end of the Shambles. Christopher Herbert settled in York in the mid-sixteenth century, was admitted to the freedom of the city in 1551, and elected a member of the Merchant Adventurers Company in the same year. In 1557 he purchased the house from the company for under £55. He was a Sheriff in 1567 and Lord Mayor in 1573. He died in 1590. His great grandson Sir Thomas Herbert was born here in 1606 and he became a close friend of King Charles I, accompanying him as he was led to the block. Thomas Percy, Earl of Northumberland, was executed here for his part in the rebellion of 1569. His head was set on a pole on Micklegate Bar for a couple of years and his body was buried in St Crux church.

Running down the side of the Herbert house and terminating in Fossgate is an ancient thoroughfare known for more than two centuries as Lady Peckett's Yard. John Peckett was Lord Mayor in 1702 and died in 1707: his wife continued to live in his pavement house after his death with the courtesy title Lady Peckett in accordance with ancient custom which said:

'He is Lord Mayor for a year and a day
But she is a Lady for ever and aye.'

A weekly market were once held in Pavement but this was moved to Parliament Street (on your right) on 16 June 1836 and transferred from there to Newgate in 1964. A one-day revival with fifty stalls was held on 31 March 1984 to maintain the council's right to hold a market here. On the left is Piccadilly which is of modern origin.

Coppergate Walk and the Jorvik Centre

Cross Parliament Street at the traffic lights to the church of **All Saints (37)**. The most notable feature is the lofty octagonal open lantern tower. Records say that 'anciently a large lamp hung in it, which was lighted in the night time, as a mark for travellers to aim at in their passage over the immense Forest of Galtres to the city'. Inside are preserved the lenses of a later version. A light still burns there nightly as a memorial to the dead of two world wars. Note the curious ornate sanctuary door-knocker which is a rare specimen.

The church was first mentioned in the Domesday Book when the Bishop of Durham held the patronage of the rectory. The registers begin in 1554 and are complete. The pulpit, with sounding board, is dated 1634 and the lectern, from the demolished St Crux, is a fine example of fifteenth century woodwork. It has long been connected with municipal and guild life of the city — thirty-nine Lord Mayors are buried here. The will boards around the pillars make fascinating reading.

With the knocker behind you turn left and sharp left again along the side of the church towards Coppergate, a name which appears as far back as 1120. One suggestion is that it is derived from an Old Scandinavian word *Koppari* meaning joiner or turner — but a more likely alternative is the Danish *koopen* 'to bargain', and that it is 'the merchants street'. The bookshop on your right stands on the site of the former Corn Market, built 1926 and closed in 1946.

Cross Coppergate and continue forward along Coppergate Walk to the **Jorvik Centre (38)** which recreates Viking York (AD876-1069) in spectacular fashion and displays five hundred artifacts unearthed from below your feet. The most remarkable find here was a Saxon helmet dating from AD700 to 750 inscribed: *In Nomine Dni Nostri Ihv Scs Sps Di Et Omnibus Amen Oshere Xpi* meaning 'In the name of our God, of Jesus and the Holy Spirit, we say Amen to God and all people, Oshere'.

On your right you will see inscribed 'This plaque commemorates the visit of HRH The Prince of Wales KG, KT, GCB to the Coppergate Development and the Jorvik Viking Centre on Thursday 17th May 1984'.

Ahead is St Mary's Square but you should turn right alongside what was originally **St Mary's Church (39)** with the tallest steeple in the city, to join Castlegate.

> ☐ *You have now covered about half the walk and you have an opportunity either to continue for the full distance or to reduce the circuit. For the complete walk turn now to page 28. However, if you prefer the shorter walk continue from here and you will rejoin the main route at page 37.*

Turn right along Castlegate past the inn with the rare sign of **Little John (40)** to the junction with Clifford Street which runs to your left.

On the opposite side of Clifford Street, with its entrance around the corner in Cumberland Street, is the **Grand Opera House (41)** which was converted from a Corn Exchange opened on 28 October 1868. It began its new role as a theatre in 1902 with the pantomime *Red Riding Hood*. Two years later Charlie Chaplin trod the boards in a Sherlock Holmes dramatisation. It closed in 1956 and reopened after a £4 million restoration on 26 September 1989.

Nessgate is said to get its name from an old word for the triangular headland between the rivers Ouse and Foss, and Castlegate, which is the setting for a seventeenth century ballad which goes:

Oh, there was a wife in Castlegate, but I won't tell of her name,
For she is both krick and kussom and she likes the fumbling game.

Bear right across the junction with Coppergate to go along Nessgate. Set into the wall of **Waterstones Bookshop (42)** on your right is a replica of a section of a tablet which reads:

HERCULI
PERPET
AETERN
EBURAC
RESTITV

Clock on St. Michael's Church

The tablet was found on this site in 1843 and conjecturally completed it refers to the restoration of a temple dedicated to Hercules AD350.

Only a few strides brings you to another junction — High Ousegate to the right, Spurriergate ahead, and Low Ousegate to the left. Stay on the right and walk across High Ousegate and Spurriergate.

The width of High Ousegate is an indication of what the breadth of the original Ouse Bridge was. Low Ousegate was widened when the present bridge was erected (1810-1820) to conform to the increased width, but High Ousegate remains in its original narrowness. In the eighteenth and nineteenth centuries it seems many young gentlemen found elegant apartments on the left hand side and tea merchants congregated on the right.

Spurriergate, as its name implies, was the street of the spur makers.

On the corner is the church of **St Michael (43)** which is said to have been given by William the Conqueror to St Mary's Abbey. The catalogue of rectors goes back to 1255. Notice the ornate clock on the wall facing Low Ousegate. There was formerly a row of houses between St Michael's and Low Ousegate which stands on what was originally part of the churchyard, but in 1734 the corner house was taken down and the entrance to Low Ousegate widened to make a more convenient turn for the stage-coaches to and from the Black Swan in Coney Street on their four day journey to London.

Keeping St Michael's on your right, walk forward a few paces and look across the road to your left and upwards. Over the row of shops you will see **two cats (44)** — one arch-backed ginger tom and the other a stalking black pussy — apparently climbing up the walls. The stone felines are reputed to have been put up by Sir Stephen Aitcheson, owner of a chain of grocers shops, in the 1920s. They may have been decorations, advertising leftovers, or perhaps a throwback to earlier days when warehouses in the area had stone cats intended to frighten away rats! Just a few more strides and you are alongside the River Ouse.

King's Staith. The Ouse in flood

Orders issued by the Mayor and Commonality of the City in the fourteenth century throw an interesting light on some of the unpleasant habits of our forefathers. One in 1371 enacted that 'No butchers of the city nor their servants shall throw refuse or offal that comes from their beasts into the River Ouse as between the bridge of Ouse and Friars minor (the Franciscan Friary that adjoined the eastern bank south of the bridge) on pain of a fine of half a mark; that no citizens shall wash skins without hair in the river; nor in any other place where the water is drawn for brewing or baking; no refuse of pigs, or offal, or other noisome stuff shall be thrown into the water, on pain of paying the fine above mentioned.' A similar order six years later included orders that 'No men of the city shall take their horses to drink the waters of the Ouse out of hand, driving them before them, which is a great peril to children playing within the city; the owner shall pay to the commonality sixpence, unless it has escaped.'

On the south side of the bridge is King's Staith which for centuries, but chiefly from the eleventh to the fifteenth, was the centre of the city's commerce. Here

Old Ouse Bridge

came ships from every continental port between Danzig and Bordeaux. Before them came the Danish merchants, and even earlier passed the ships of the Classis Britannica bearing supplies for the Sixth Legion which garrisoned the fortress, bringing fresh troops and taking home officials who had served their contract.

Hard by the bridge is the ancient **Kings Arms (45)** which has also borne the name Ouse Bridge Inn and has always suffered the inundations of the river — a fact commemorated in the bar with a plaque showing the heights reached by the waters.

Cross the river by Ouse Bridge. As early as the eleventh century there was some structure here, possibly the wooden one which fell in 1154. Eighty years later Archbishop Walter de Gray granted a warrant authorising the building of a stone replacement. The bridge, built in 1235, lasted three hundred years, but disaster overtook it in 1564 when a heavy fall of snow and severe frost with a sudden thaw produced so much water and floating ice that the centre two arches collapsed and in the fall twelve houses were overthrown and twelve people drowned. It had consisted of six narrow arches, and ships had to lower their mast to go up river. It was crowded with buildings of every kind — shops, tenements, chantry chapel, and a gaol. Shops and tenements were revenue producers for the maintenance fund. The chapel, dedicated to St William, was erected in 1268 at the expense of the city in atonement for an affray which took place on the bridge between the retinue of John Comyn, a Scottish nobleman, and a band of citizens, in which some of the Scotsmen were killed. The buildings included a hall in which for centuries city fathers assembled to transact their business, while below was the common gaol. This collection of

buildings stood on the north side at the western end — across on your right. In 1566 the bridge was restored over a period of fourteen years, and in the late eighteenth century it once again needed attention. However, a new bridge was constructed — begun in 1810 and completed in 1820. It was a toll bridge for the first nine years of its life, being made free in June 1829. The first vehicle to pass over without paying toll was carrying a load of timber for Minster repairs following a disastrous fire started by the arsonist Jonathan Martin.

Ahead is Bridge Street which was originally Ouse Bridge End, probably because it was difficult to say where the bridge ended and the crowded buildings began — but in 1810 the houses on the north side were taken down and the street widened to become New Bridge Street, although the 'New' wore off at some point.

Turn right alongside the chemist store immediately you have crossed the bridge to enter the riverside walk *and then rejoin the main route which continues on page 37.*

☐ **Continue from here if you are following the complete walk.**

St Mary's existed here long before the Norman Conquest, with a list of rectors going back to 1267, but it now houses the **Heritage Centre (46)**, containing the most fascinating and helpful displays showing the evolution of the city and its architecture. Rich tapestries, a diorama of the River Ouse and Ouse Bridge as it might have looked in 1300, models of buildings, and even the restored stonework of the eleventh century church with its superb stained glass. A glittering collection of gold and silver regalia, civic plate and tableware is also displayed.

St Mary's – now the Heritage Centre

Centre-piece is a restored gilded sea-horse which once adorned the Victorian Sea Horse Inn in Fawcett Street until it closed in 1947.

Turn left and walk forward. On the right is **Castlegate House (47)** designed by architect John Carr (1723-1807) for Peter Johnson, Recorder of York, and completed in 1763. It was the site of the Mount Friendly Girls School from 1831 to 1857.

A few strides to your left is **Fairfax House (48)**, completed in 1762 to the plans of John Carr for Viscount Fairfax of Elmley, now restored to house a million pounds worth of Georgian furniture and an outstanding collection of clocks. The Library ceiling embodies portrait medallions of Milton, Addison, Locke and Pope. Elsewhere, in a swirl of delicate patterns created by Italian plasterer Joseph Cortere, you can discern individual feathers on his birds and even play an original eighteenth century tune from notes he impressed in plasterwork sheets of music. In the pediment surmounting the imposing frontage is an elaborate stone cartouche with a circular window.

Clifford's Tower

Turn right at the end where you are confronted by a car park and Clifford's Tower and walk down Tower Street.

It was from the battlements of **Clifford's Tower (49)** that Roger de Clifford was hanged in 1322. The night of Friday 16 March 1190 was *Shabbat Ha Gadol* — the Great Sabbath — when a hundred and fifty Jews, having sought protection in the tower from a mob incited by Richard Malebisse and others, chose to die at each other's hands rather than renounce their faith. Those who tried to escape were butchered in what has been described as 'the worst and most deplorable outrage ever perpetrated within the City of York'. In these riots the wooden Norman keep was destroyed. The stone structure erected to replace it dates from the middle of the thirteenth century. The stone keep was damaged by fire in 1644 during the Civil War, restored, and again seriously damaged by an explosion in 1684 when the roof was destroyed. The quatrefoil shaped towers give good views of the surroundings.

Adjacent is **York Castle Museum (50)** which was opened in 1938. Notice the Dick Turpin painted silhouette sign which points the way to one of the city's most famous attractions.

Originally two prisons, the museum owes its existence to Dr John L Kirk of Pickering who built up a collection of horse brasses, fire insurance signs, furniture, farming equipment, and even shop fronts which in 1935 he offered to York. The council agreed to house the collection in the disused women's prison, built by the architect John Carr who also designed the Assize Courts which stand opposite. The collection took three years to transport to York, and over the years has taken over the Debtors' Prison, completed in 1705 and generally attributed to Sir John Vanburgh, one of the Country's leading architects whose achievements include Castle Howard and Blenheim Palace. Apart from the various collections, the most famous exhibits are the re-created streets of Kirkgate, Alderman's Walk, Princess Mary Court, and Half Moon Court. Period rooms, music, hearth, agricultural and other galleries provide unique displays of York and district 'bygones'. The more or less oval shaped expanse of grass in front is called the *Eye of York*.

The **Assize Courts (51)** were erected in 1777 and in them or their predecessors have been held some notable trials including those of Richard Turpin (1739), Eugene Aram (1759), the Luddites (1812), and the Peterloo rioters (1820).

Cross Tower Street, formerly called Castlegate Postern Lane, at the zebra crossing to the short length of city wall which faces St George's Fields. At its riverside end stood Davy Tower, similar to the one you will encounter later near Lendal Bridge, and at the end nearest the Castle stood Castlegate Postern. This was a narrow gateway leading from the city into St George's Field, but the postern was taken down in 1826-7.

The land on the city side of the wall between the right and castle, extending

Fishergate Postern

about halfway to Ouse Bridge once formed the site of a Franciscan friary established about 1230 and continued until the Suppression in 1539. All that remains are a few fragments built into walls in Tower Street and the Friars Wall along the riverside, which you will see clearly from Skeldergate Bridge. These remnants serve to remind us of the magnificent buildings in which a Parliament of Edward II met in 1322, in which the Parliaments of Edward III assembled, where the king invariably resided during all his visits to York, and in which Richard II once stayed. Imagine the activities, pageants, tragedies and vital scenes in English history which have been enacted here!

Behind the wall is **Tower Place (52)**, one of the city's most secluded residential rows dating from around 1830.

Behind iron railings and fixed to a wall is a **plaque (53)** overlooked by most people. It is the official flood marker recording the heights reached by the swollen River Ouse.

St George's Field (54) has belonged to the citizens from time immemorial. Here every citizen enjoyed the right to 'walk, shoot with bow and arrow, and to dry linen'. Originally bounded by the Rivers Ouse and Foss, the Castle moat, and the city wall from Castlegate Postern to Davy Tower on the riverside, much was lost in the nineteenth century construction of Tower Street and the eastern approaches to Skeldergate Bridge.

Here, until 1607, was kept the cucking, or ducking, stool for the punishment of female offenders. Originally inflicted upon women who used false measures or brewed bad beer, it was later used for those ladies who indulged in scolding. They were subjected to the painful and degrading spectacle of being fastened in the ducking stool and plunged three times into the river.

Walk diagonally across the open space to the foot of Skeldergate Bridge where you will see a short flight of stone steps which you climb to the roadway above. To your left is Castle Mills Bridge over the River Foss which has its confluence with the River Ouse a few hundred yards below Skeldergate Bridge. Just across Castle Mills Bridge is **Fishergate Postern (55)**, a massive, square, stone building which was constructed to form the terminal defence of this section of the city walls, either when they were first built of stone in the thirteenth century or a

31

century later when they were restored. At the time of its erection the waters of the Foss extended to its base — a practice they sometimes seem to try to repeat!

Turn right on to Skeldergate Bridge — youngest of four bridges in the city over the River Ouse. Immediately on your right is the **old toll house (56)**. The bridge was formally declared free from tolls on 1 April 1914 by the Lord Mayor. The foundation stone of the bridge was laid on 12 June 1878, it was first used for pedestrians on 1 January 1881, and it was formally opened for general traffic on 10 March 1881. There are extensive views both up and down the river, with the stones of the former Franciscan friary, now embodied in other walls, being easily identified on the right hand side as you look up river.

The Ouse Bridge — the oldest crossing — makes a striking picture, especially at evening time when it is floodlit. Across the bridge on your left is Bishopgate Street but known to most older residents as Cherry Hill. Beside it, on a site once occupied by a distillery and, about 1850, a chemical manure works, is the Bishops Wharf development of luxury flats.

To your right alongside the bridge are the steps to the **old ferry (57)**, which did duty for untold years before the bridge was built. The open landing next to the steps was, from 1816 to 1875, the scene of the daily departure and arrival of steamers carrying passengers to and from Selby, Goole and Hull — for this was the ordinary means of travel to these places throughout that period. The first of these vessels — they made the journey to Hull in about eight hours and returned according to the tide — was *The Waterloo* which ran a trial trip on 25 April 1816.

Dominating the corner is the **restaurant (58)** opened in 1981 in the restored bonded warehouse which Lord Esher in his report on York described as

Skeldergate Bridge

Restaurant in the old Bonding Warehouse

'outstandingly handsome'. When it originally opened on 26 May 1875 business was so brisk that another, about double the size, was built next to it a year later.

The site chosen for these warehouses had been the centre of the city's commerce in the Middle Ages, being next to the Old Crane Wharf. The 'old crane' was augmented by a new one in the 1770s. Charges for using the Old Crane appear regularly in the city's accounts in the fifteenth century, and give a good idea of the diversity of goods moved along the river — wine, woad, madder, alum, spices, grain, salt, wax, steel, iron, linen, sea-coal and lead.

On the piece of garden in front of the warehouse stood, until it was demolished in 1808, Skeldergate Postern, and a wall led down to a tower on the river bank to face Davy Tower, or Friars Minor Tower, as it was sometimes called, on the other side of the river.

Ignore the steps on your right down to Skeldergate and walk forward a few yards, carefully crossing Cromwell Road to Baile Hill ahead, which marks the end of another section of the city walls.

Baile Hill (59) is the twin mound of Clifford's Tower on the opposite side of the river, which you have already seen. The two were obviously built to command the passage by river and are essentially Danish in conception. They

Baile Hill

were probably built between AD867 and 927. There was a wooden castle on top in Norman times which was badly damaged in the fighting of 1069. Baile Hill passed into the possession of the Archbishops of York about 1200, and about 1460, after a dispute about maintenance, it was acquired by the city. Later it was used for grazing cattle, for musters of armed citizens, for archery practice, and for traditional Shrove Tuesday games. A gaol was built here in 1802-7 but demolished in 1880 when houses were built nearby.

According to a record of the time the stone gaol was 'erected on an elegant and extensive scale, reflecting much honour on the city and the architect'. As a result an ancient narrow lane was called Gaol Lane, but with subsequent enlargement became the Cromwell Road you are standing in today — although Oliver Cromwell seems never to have had any connection whatever with this district. Leave Baile Hill behind you, staying on the left and walk down the slight slope into Skeldergate.

Novelist and friend of Charles Dickens, Wilkie Collins chose this as a setting in his lesser known book *No Name*. He was not very thrilled, however, for he wrote: 'The few old houses left in the street are disguised in melancholy modern costume of whitewash and cement. Shops of the smaller and poorer order intermixed here and there with dingy warehouses and joyless private residences of red brick comprise the present aspect of Skeldergate'.

Skeldergate does not appear in any records until 1170, but there can be no doubt the street is far older than that. One suggestion is that it was the street of the shield makers but more likely it is derived from a Scandinavian word meaning to unload, and in view of the age-long business of shipping here this looks more probable.

When the Franciscans across the river obtained permission to build their enclosing wall in 1291, one side of which encroached on the high water level of the then tidal river, Skeldergate merchants feared with good reason that such a structure might lead to silting of the river. Accordingly, in 1305, they obtained permission to protect their frontages with a similar wall. The wall then built still constitutes the river front of the wharfs and warehouses, despite the fact that many of the latter have been demolished between Skeldergate Bridge and

Queen's Staith. There are references to Skeldergate merchants in 1486 and 1661 and many in later times, all testifying to the extensive trading activity here.

To your right is the Castle Mills development of sheltered homes for the elderly completed in 1990. On your left, at the corner of Carr's Lane, stands **Dame Middleton's Hospital (60)** — now converted into a hotel. Built and endowed in 1659 by Dame Anne Middleton, wife of Peter Middleton, Sheriff of York, it was originally founded as a hostel for the widows of twenty freemen, and in 1829 was rebuilt and enlarged at the expense of the Corporation. A stone effigy of the foundress stands over the entrance. Alongside is a row of almshouses with a colourful stone crest on the end wall and the inscription 'These almshouses were erected by public subscription to the memory of the late Sir Joseph Terry 1899'.

York's famous architect John Carr is commemorated by Carr's Lane, formerly Church Lane. The house which he built and lived in for many years was bombed in August 1942 at which time the street name was changed.

Effigy of Dame Middleton

Only a few more yards forward on your left, sandwiched between Albion Street and Cumberland Street is the **Cock and Bottle Inn (61)**. Here stood the Plumbers Arms, a timber framed building of about 1575 with a sixteenth century fireplace, seventeenth century panelling and a fine eighteenth century staircase. It was taken down in 1965 but many of its features were retained in the new inn which is reputed to be haunted by the ghost of the Duke of Buckingham since it stands in the garden of his former town house. Described by Alexander

Crest on the almshouse

Queen's Staith

Pope as 'chemist, fiddler, statesman and buffoon', the Duke (1627-88) was said to have had a laboratory here where he was seeking the secret of transmuting base metals into gold.

Turn right across the road and walk down to Queen's Staith — partner of King's Staith across the river. About the time of the building of Ouse Bridge a new staith was thought necessary on the south bank of the river and so Queen's Staith came into existence (1810-1815). It was first used for landing coal and was known as Coal Staith. Notice the tall, redundant warehouses and cranes recalling more prosperous days — barges still unload here from time to time. The heyday of the earlier wharf began after 1660 when Alderman Christopher Topham, who was Lord Mayor that year, was instrumental in arranging the construction of a public wharf which for many years was called Topham's Staith. It was enlarged in 1678, and in the eighteenth century when there was an extensive trade in butter from Yorkshire to London it was a hive of activity, but by the beginning of the nineteenth century it was 'almost destroyed and forgotten'.

Look across the river to the Kings Arms Inn with its pictorial sign showing the head and shoulders of Richard III and his coat of arms — last of the Yorkist Kings before the House of Tudor.

At the corner of the staith and Cumberland Street is **Cumberland House (62)**, a fine Georgian building erected in the eighteenth century by Alderman William Cornwell, a brewer who was city Sheriff in 1700 and Lord Mayor in 1712 and 1725. It appears to have been given its name in honour of the Duke of Cumberland, second son of George II who visited York in 1746.

Climb the steps and cross the road to join the riverside walk between the chemist's shop and river — the chemist's should be on your left.

□ *Rejoin the main route here if you have taken the shorter walk.*

On what was formerly a dingy warehouse and a coal, sand and gravel merchant's wharf has arisen the striking **Viking Hotel (63)**, opened 10 January 1969, which resulted in the creation of the first part of the riverside walk. At the corner of the hotel, outside the Buttery Bar, a seat commemorates Mr Edwin Sherwood Piercy, owner of a fertiliser factory which also stood here. The business was founded in 1770 and Mr Piercy, a native of Sunderland, used to receive raw materials from Germany in barges. He died in 1967 and was one of the first in York to have a car.

On the end wall of the hotel is a plaque 'To the Memory of John Snow 1813-1850 Pioneer Anaesthetist and epidemiologist. Born near here'. When ether and chloroform were introduced in 1846 and 1847 Dr Snow taught himself how to use them safely and gave over 4,000 chloroform anaesthetics without a death. Among his patients was Queen Victoria who, after the birth of Prince

All Saints Church

Leopold and Princess Beatrix wrote in her diary 'Dr Snow gave that blessed chloroform and the effect was soothing, quieting and delightful'.

Here too, in 1970, two pairs of swans, given by the Dyers and Vintners Livery Company to the city were released into the river by the Duchess of Kent. This point is also believed to have marked the spot of the Dublin Stones. Hereabouts, in medieval times, a narrow lane called 'Develynstanes' led from North Street to the river. The name derives from *Dyflinn* the Scandinavian name for Dublin. The city was the centre of Viking activity in England north of the Humber from AD867 until the death of king Eric Bloodaxe in 954. A line of communication existed between Dublin and Scandinavia across northern England by way of York, possibly reaching the river at this point.

Alongside are the **Joseph Rowntree Gardens (64)** which were presented to the city in 1959 as a perpetual open space.

Across the river can be seen the former home of the city's newspapers which have been published since 1759, although the first newspaper, the *York Courant*, went on sale on 27 February 1719. Beside it is the Guildhall which we shall meet later in the walk.

Walk around to the front of the hotel which faces North Street — a name going back as far as 1090 when it appears in the form of Nordstreta, but its origins are obscure.

Cross North Street and walk up the narrow paved way alongside **All Saints Church (65)** to the entrance. It is the finest of York's many medieval churches with architecture of the twelfth, thirteenth, fourteenth and fifteenth centuries. The fine stained glass of fourteenth and fifteenth centuries is exceptional, and the fifteenth century hammer-beam roofs with splendid

All Saints Church. Medieval carving

38

bosses, carved wooden figures of angels playing musical instruments or holding emblems, are excellent examples of medieval wood carving. Notice also the pulpit (1675), the mayoral board of the eighteenth century containing names of parishioners who became Lord Mayor of the city, and the eighteenth century benefactions board.

In eleven windows is some of the finest medieval parish church glass in York and it ranks among the best in England. The six corporal acts of mercy according to the Gospel of St Matthew are shown in a window of c.1410, and next to this is the fifteenth century *Pricke of Conscience* window, so called because it depicts the last fifteen days of the world as described in a medieval poem called *The Pricke of Conscience*. The spire is floodlit at night.

All Saints Church. Detail from the 'Pricke of Conscience' window

Beside the church at the back is the Anchorage, restored in 1987 and once claimed to be the smallest house in England. An Anchorage was a placed where a religious recluse lived — anchorite if a man, anchoress if a woman. This one was believed to have been built soon after the First World War by Ridsdale Tate and it contains a 'squint' through which the recluse could see the altar in the church.

Retrace your steps to North Street and on the corner are three **fifteenth century cottages (66)** which have been renovated. The old building with the carved corner post is believed to be all that remains of a Dominican friary which stood here from 1228 to 1539.

Turn left up Tanner Row which is more or less on the line of the old Roman road to Tadcaster. It is thought that a ford here went across the river through the Porta Praetoria and past the Mansion House where our walk started.

The junction ahead is of Rougier Street to your right and George Hudson Street to your left. Rougier Street is the point from which most bus services radiate. Its somewhat unusual name recalls the fact that Joseph Rougier, comb maker, established his works close by here at the end of the eighteenth century or early in the nineteenth century, and the business was carried on by his family until about 1900. Rougier Street was built between 1838 and 1846.

In the autumn of 1840 the railway authorities began to urge the corporation to build a new and wider approach to the railway station — then situated in

York Minster and the city walls

Toft Green — to avoid the inconvenience of the narrow circuitous route through North Street and Tanner Row. After three years of negotiation about cost the construction of Railway Street was carried out. At first it was called Hudson Street, in compliment to the Railway King, but when in 1849 his grandiose schemes collapsed with a resultant financial loss to many people it was changed in response to public clamour. However, the entrepreneur has been forgiven and his rehabilitation came on 14 December 1971, the 100th anniversary of his death.

Cross the road to proceed further up Tanner Row past the **Great Northern Inn (67)**. This was refurbished in 1984 to replace the former Pageant Inn, the name of which commemorated the great Corpus Christi parade which, in medieval times, came this way.

Dominating everything hereabouts is the great office complex of the former **North Eastern Railway (68)**, surmounted by its huge weather-vane of a steam locomotive. Walk around the iron railings on your right, designed to ensure that only pedestrians pass this way into the courtyard of this great building which was erected in 1907.

On your left are other railway offices but of much greater age, for this was the original York railway station.

The York and North Midland Railway Company was established at a meeting held in the Guildhall on 10 October 1835 with Alderman George Hudson as its chairman and George Stephenson as its engineer. They purchased about four acres from the corporation and opened their station on it on 4 January 1841.

Walk forward and you will see on your left the fine Portland Stone **war memorial (69)** designed by Sir Edwin Lutyens. Weighing more than 1,000 tons, it was built by the North Eastern Railway Company in honour of 2,236 railmen from the eastern half of England killed in the First World War. It was unveiled on 16 June 1924 by Marshal Lord Plumer, and since its sixtieth anniversary, when 550 names of railmen killed in World War Two and other campaign were added, it has been floodlit.

Cross the road carefully and mount the steps to rejoin the traffic-free path along the walls, running parallel to Station Road. Look over the wall to your left, having turned right at the top of the steps so that you are facing the distant towers of the Minster.

Below is the statue of **George Leeman (70)** who gave his name to the road immediately in front which was once called Thief Lane. He was three times Lord Mayor, elected Member of Parliament in 1865, 1871 and 1874, as well as being chairman of the North Eastern Railway Company. Below on your

George Leeman

Arms of the North Eastern Railway

right are the floral creations designed by the corporation as a foil to the walls.

Across the road is the headquarters of the North Eastern Region of British Rail — a thought far from the minds of its designers William Bell and Horace Field.

Attracting attention is a colourful crest. The badges are of the York and North Midland Railway, left, and the York, Newcastle and Berwick Railway, right, which formed the North Eastern Railway in 1854 and in 1923 became part of the London and North Eastern Railway.

Unhampered by traffic you cross the archway over the junction with Rougier Street on your right and descend to the edge of Lendal Bridge. Ahead and below is **Barker Tower (71)** (or North Street Postern). It was a mortuary and a toll-gate in the fourteenth century and more recently a crafts centre. Chains are said to

Lendal Tower

have been hung across the river to **Lendal Tower (72)**, so preventing boats from slipping away without paying dues and obstructing unwelcome visitors. According to an 1890 year-book: 'In the year 1662 during the reign of Charles II, waterworks were first established in the Lendal Tower, York. A pumping engine worked by two horses was placed in the tower by means of which a scanty supply of water was furnished the citizens every week.

Lamps on Lendal Bridge

'The mains at that time were trunks of trees hollowed out and fastened together and laid down in the streets. This went on for nearly a century when the works were purchased by Col. Thornton who made considerable improvements. At his death a steam engine was introduced . . .'. The waterworks premises are still there.

To your right alongside the river is the site of a **Roman temple (73)** erected c. AD180 which may possibly have been dedicated to the pagan gods Jupiter and Bacchus. During excavations in 1989 more than 1,000 bronze Roman coins, a second century gold ear-ring, a jet signet ring with an engraving of a swan as a seal, a fourth century figure thought to be a Roman god carved from jet, and evidence of sacrificial offerings, were discovered.

Arguments about the costs and position of Lendal Bridge raged for twenty years from 1840 before an Act of Parliament was obtained for its construction. Work started in 1860 and after a year's labour the whole contraption fell into the river killing five men. So the council had to start all over again, this time with the services of a civil engineer.

Opened on 8 January 1863, it replaced a ferry run by John Leeman since 1831. Four months later he was presented with a horse and cart and £15 in cash as compensation. To celebrate the opening the Lord Mayor entertained 120 guests at the Mansion House, while the men who had worked on the bridge sat down to their dinner in the 'outer wool shed' adjoining the cattle market. The bridge became toll free on 7 August 1894.

Notice the former **toll-house (74)** on your right, special china models of which have been created for collectors. First day's tolls yielded £4. 5s. 10d (£4.29p). Tolls were 'For every horse or beast drawing a cart or similar 2d, not drawing 1d; oxen or meat cattle 5d a score; sheep, twopence-halfpenny per score and pedestrians a halfpenny.'

The ornate bridge by Thomas Page, engineer of Westminster Bridge and a gifted designer of iron structures, is decorated with cross keys, lions and Yorkshire roses, with lamp standards surmounted by angels holding shields.

Looking up river you will see Scarborough Bridge built in 1844 to carry the York and Scarborough Railway across the river. This was the first bridge within the city boundaries to share with Ouse Bridge facilities for pedestrians to cross the river. Although primarily a rail bridge it was supplemented from the beginning with a footway, originally situated in the middle between the up and down lines. In 1874 a section about eight feet wide was constructed on the south side at a lower level then the railway portion to take pedestrians, as it does today.

Walk forward and on your left at a break in the wall is Museum Gardens and the ruins of **St Mary's Abbey (75)** — the first monastic house to be established in Yorkshire after the Norman Conquest. It became one of the largest and wealthiest of the Benedictine Abbeys with a mitred abbot who sat in the House of Lords. Founded about 1080 by Stephen of Lastingham, it was later enlarged by King William Rufus who refounded it as St Mary's Abbey. It was suppressed in 1540. Most of the precinct walls built in the middle of the thirteenth century by Abbot Simon of Warwick still stand. Here are held the famous Mystery Plays — the pageant of medieval times. Near the entrance are the remains of the hospital of St Leonard whose riverside landing was down the narrow lane to the left. It is conjectured that Lendal arose from a slurred rendering of St Leonard's Lendynge Hill.

Ruins of St Mary's Abbey

44

Carved head of Aesculapius, the god of healing

The **Yorkshire Museum (76)**, built by the Yorkshire Philosophical Society in 1828 to house their archaeological, natural history, and geological collections, was handed over to the city in 1961. It contains rich finds from Roman York and houses, among other outstanding objects, the Anglian Ormside Bowl and the unique thirteenth century statues from St Mary's Abbey. Remains, too, of some of the conventional buildings are preserved, including wall foundations and column bases of the Chapter House vestibule, the Chapter House entrance, and the fire-place of the warming house.

Cross the road to your right into Lendal and walk on the left. Only a few strides brings you to a building of unusual design, now a hotel but until 1979 the **lodging of H.M. Judges of Assize (77)**. It served this function from 1806. Over the door is the carved head of Aesculapius, the god of healing. The house stands on the former site of the church of St Wilfred and was built about 1720 by Dr Clifton Wintringham (1689-1748), a well known physician and author of some works of medicine. He was the father of Sir Clifton Wintringham, a physician to George III.

Napoleon

A little further down you will be greeted by the colourful 5ft 4in high figure of **Napoleon (78)** outside a tobacconist shop. Carved in 1880 and believed to be one of three imported into Hull and sold for £50 each, he is a rare effigy trade sign, once offering a pinch of snuff to passers-by. Letters simply addressed to 'Napoleon, York' are delivered without delay, and his chequered career has seen him dumped into the Ouse more than once by high-spirited revellers.

On the right hand side stands the Post Office and **Lendal Cellars (79)** on the site of an Augustinian Friary with its library of 646 books. The Friary was established in 1268 and suppressed in 1538. Richard, Duke of Gloucester, was received there by the Lord Mayor in 1482.

Lendal Cellars, opened as a wine bar in 1984, incorporates a restored section of the Friary wall and a well believed to have been first built by the friars.

First records of a post office in the city date back to 1700. In 1734 the Lendal Post Office was opened, extended in 1884, and modernised in 1984. In the 1884 extensions the post office replaced a three-storey eighteenth century house built right up to the Mansion house. It was the home of Postmaster William Oldfield who was also a prosperous wine merchant. He was twice Lord Mayor and he gave a sumptuous banquet at the Mansion House on 23 April 1825 to celebrate the King's birthday of which he recorded: 'Upon this occasion instead of illumination by candles and transparencies, the Mansion House was illuminated by gas outside, by the letters G IV R, the size of the letters being three-and-a-half feet. The expense of the illumination to me £NIL.'

A little further forward on your right is a former medieval alley-way which led to a landing stage and the Roman ford. Romans came this way from Tadcaster to enter the Praetorian Gate, and limestone for the Minster was hauled up Stonegate, which probably accounts for its name.

Walk down it to the **Guildhall (80)**, a replica of a fifteenth century building built on the site of a former Commonhall. Each oak pillar is cut from a single tree trunk, the original ones being taken from the Forest of Galtres to the north. The roof bosses are copies of former bosses depicting heraldic shields, grotesques and foliage. At the apex are the Royal Arms and the Arms of York. The stained glass window depicts the history of York. To the left of the dais is a wrought-iron balustrade given by York's twin city of Münster, Germany. To the right is a bronze plaque, dated 18 July 1924, presented by the City of New York 'as an expression of friendship and goodwill'.

The Guildhall

The Guildhall has served many purposes apart from providing a meeting place for the guilds. Meetings, concerts, exhibitions and the like are still held here and in 1971 the first dinner for over thirty years was arranged to celebrate the Silver Jubilee of York Civic Trust. Probably the most spectacular occasion was in 1483 when Richard III was entertained there on his first visit as King. He is honoured by an inscribed plaque presented by the Society of Friends of Richard III during the quincentenary celebrations of 1983 which reads:

King Richard the Third, 1483-1485. In commemoration of King Richard III Duke of Gloucester and Lord of the North and of his "great labour, good and benevolent lordship" for the honour of this city. MOST FAMOUS PRINCE OF BLESSED MEMORY.

Perhaps they should have added that during his visit of 29 August 1483 he reduced the city's taxes from £140 to £5 11s. 2d!

Now retrace your steps to St Helen's Square and you will find yourself back at the Mansion House where our walk began.

The Guildhall at night